Stamatis Polenakis

Birds In The Night

Translated from the Greek by
Richard Pierce

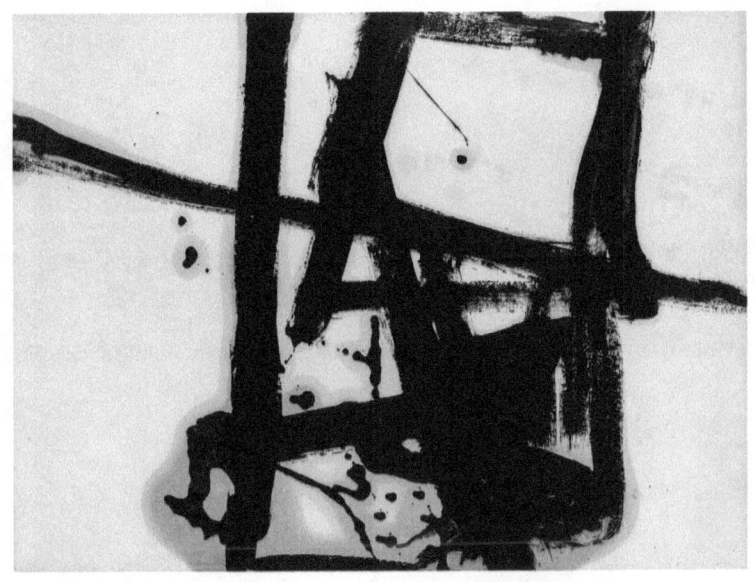

SPUYTEN DUYVIL
New York City

Cover image : Franz Kline, *Black and White*, 1956. Oil on Paper, 19 1/2" X 25 1/4".

Library of Congress Control Number: 2024944332

I first became familiar with the extraordinary work of Stamatis Polenakis during the period from the fall of 2018 through the end of 2019, when he was translating my poetry book *Pythagoras in Love* from English into Greek with remarkable fluency and eloquence. Thanks to the insight and wisdom of Athens poet and philosopher Ginger F. Zaimis, who had introduced us, I learned of Polenakis's singular and exceptional poetry at the same time, especially in his 2017 book *The Roses of Mercedes*, which had been the co-winner of the Greek National Prize for Poetry in that year.

Subsequently, I read some of the early poems of what became *Birds in the Night* with great excitement, and even tried, despite my challenged Greek, my hand at translating them. I was struck by the power of these poems' vision, their brooding and sometimes stunning landscapes, and their stark eloquence and depth of language, from this early stage on.

As mentioned in the preface to the first book to receive the Daniel Hoffman Legacy Book Prize, *Shades & Graces* by the distinguished poet, critic, and neurosurgeon Michael Salman, I am the executor of the Daniel Hoffman Archive at the US Library of Congress in Washington DC, and the arbiter of the Legacy Prize. There is no formal submission process for it, but I rely on my many years experience in the field of poetry, and an extensive network of global contacts, to make a selection that best exemplifies the brilliant critical judgement, and profound knowledge of Dr. Hoffman, who was (among many distinguished credentials) Poet Laureate of the United States under its predecessor title Consultant in Poetry to the Library of Congress, in the 1973-74 academic year.

As I became better acquainted with Polenakis's work over the past several years, I realized that he is an incomparable poet, (though largely unknown in America), whose work is so compelling that recognition for it can only enhance the stature of American poetry as well as that of Greece, rooted as American poetry is through the cultures of both England and Renaissance Europe in the fountainhead nation of all Western poetry and literature, Greece.

I will briefly discuss the first poems of *Birds in the Night*, both to give a sense of the highly original art in them, and to prepare the reader for the entire book that lies beyond them. Let me mention at the outset the wonderful and eloquent quality of the English translation by Richard Pierce, which has a great clarity, ease, and authenticity of detail and idiom in it, despite challenges often faced by translators from Greek into English. Tod Thilleman, the series editor, continues to bring his energy, commitment, and love of poetry to the project.

Mystery, striking imagery, and a fearsome atmosphere are recurring motifs in all the poems of *Birds*. Even the briefest glance at the first poem affects the reader forcefully along these lines: "the darkness emerging from behind the hills," "purple hair streaming" (a recurring image)…"the air raid sirens began to sound again and we crawl like blind animals into the stifling shelters." There is no specificity as to time and place, but a sense of menace and inevitable doom permeates the language, unnerving the reader even as she or he is riveted to numerous startling images. Such images recur in the next poem: "bumping against the cold sides of the well like blind animals…I saw your purple hair streaming." Then a great and emphatic line comes, with a sort of modern Shakespearean resonance in its depth: "No one has ever explained the riddle of the world."

The fiery-sky opening of this poem moves on to a "desolate coast" where "a wave hurled us to the edge of this inhospitable earth." Inhospitable, yes, and desolate, and frightening throughout, yet always Polenakis's great poetry redeems these terrifying moments with hints of human connection, love, consolation. Or, if it doesn't quite redeem them, the depth and amazing language make the reader whole in some inscrutable and archetypal way.

The following poem opens with "muddy rivers,"as we see that initial settings in these poems continue to shift: from darkness, to a sky illumined by flames, to rivers "below the dim light of the dying flame." Then, once again, words return to the surface of consciousness as if stirring from some primordial vision: "purple hair streaming." "Bushes burning…" and once again an "uninhabited earth" with "black caverns" where prophecies echo. Polenakis's immortal poetry holds the language and imagery of modern myth, created before and for our contemporary eyes, as if coming in a full dark circle from the ancient Greek origins of so much of Western myth.

I have found it a truly startling and amazing experience to read such work, created in the midst of these tumultuous and agonizing times.

"*Come, dear great soul, we call you, we're waiting for you.*"

Letter from Paul Verlaine
to Arthur Rimbaud, September 1871

"*O soul, hang your clothes on the wheel of life and death*"

Rumi, *In the Arms of the Beloved*

Whoever saw a lovely maiden being dragged by a dead man?

Traditional Greek poem

Although we were rapidly enveloped in the darkness emerging from behind the hills, we managed to find one another. In the shattered mirror I saw your purple hair streaming. Then I was afraid—now it's too late—to touch that all too frail body offered to me stark naked in the brief period of quiet granted to us before the air raid sirens began to sound again and we crawl like blind animals into the stifling shelters.

The whole sky was illuminated by flames. We descended deeper and deeper, bumping against the cold sides of the well like blind animals, trapped in an invisible snare. In the frigid moonlight, I saw your purple hair streaming. No one has ever explained the riddle of the world. We saw descending among us the frightful angel of love and death; we saw, along the desolate coast, dark and immobile gondolas. A wave hurled us to the edge of this inhospitable earth.

We go into the same muddy rivers again and again, as in a dream. Below the dim light of the dying flame, I saw your purple hair streaming. We saw the sempiternal bushes burning, we saw the dark thunderbolt of love and death fall on the uninhabited earth. *Away incurable one!; pain will be your lot*—the terrifying prophecy resounded from the black caverns of the earth.

Dawn was already breaking behind the hills of madness. Clutching the last white cloud of love, we saw the ultimate vision of the old moribund world, and we heard the voice resounding for the last time in the rocky wasteland. In the flames of the eternal lamp, there beyond the stone of tears, I saw your purple hair streaming. Tomorrow the wind shall scatter the ashes of the one who once rose from the dead.

We proceeded strenuously, elbowing our way through the panic-stricken crowd suffocating on the wharf. All around us furious throngs struggled to escape from the flames. Women tore out their hair and threw themselves into the contaminated waves. In innumerable deceptive lenses, in the mirror of our bygone happiness, I saw your purple hair streaming. Blind girl who led me to where no one has ever arrived, dark swallow and stone forever uprooted from its cradle, from the earth and the soil. No one came to our aid walking on a dead sea.

Our hands were joined in the dark. Traversing stellar distances I gently touched the large, sorrowful root, I touched these moist, disconsolate eyelids. Through the night and fog, among enormous pillars of smoke, I saw, as in a dream, your purple hair streaming. I arrived here, a poor suppliant seeking shelter, and proceeded fearlessly as far as the unknown hinterland of this unfathomable land, to the place where God still dwells. But you, forever surrendering yourself utterly to the moonlight and the starry night, you alone possessed the great mystery of fate and death.

All night long I struggled with the angel. A mere mortal, only one time did I touch your immortal hands, whiter than the goddess's. Below the demonic drumbeats of love, in the mortal darkness of the immortal world I saw your purple hair streaming. Wind was blowing from the shores. No one has ever looked at God straight in the eyes and survived.

We were walking all alone on the edge of the sea; day was breaking and our eyes were burning from the fire of the vision. We saw the silent cloudburst approaching and then, with your steady hand you showed me something that was sinking far away on the horizon. I remember that the ship was called *Don Juan*, I remember that we saw, in the azure flash of lightning, the saintly poet Shelley with his hands upraised to the sky. Before we sank forever like stones, I saw your purple hair streaming. *Away, away! to thy sad and silent home*, we heard the melody of love emerging from the pitch-black waves.

In the dazzling light of dawn, we saw the dark swallows returning. We followed the eerie music that led us far away to the fatal precipices of poetry. We returned to our starting point, waiting for the snow to fall gently on both the living and dead; the world was reborn from the ashes and everything had to be said all over again. I loved you utterly for your mysteriousness; I was never able to find out what ancestry was flowing in your veins. Leaning over the eternal wellsprings of life, I saw your purple hair streaming. I see you again today, the same as before, maiden in the night suddenly appearing from among the waves. When the dark swallows return, let us not expect a helping hand from poetry.

Through the cracked windows we saw the sea for the last time and, far away, the desolate shores and the gloomy lights of ships vanishing on the horizon. We lived exposed to the tempests of God and poetry, and since we knew that *every angel is terrifying*, it would have been vain to seek refuge in any angel or muse. Yet I followed you to the end and touched your sacred nudity. In the mirror of the past, present and future I saw your purple hair streaming. I followed you, burrowing deeper and deeper into mother's icy embrace, as far as the unknown dominion of the tempest and the wind that uproots the trees and lifts the cosmic waves. As far as the abode of God and of language, which destroys and self-destructs.

The heat of your body kept us both alive as we lay under the snow. In the hazy twilight of our last night I saw your purple hair streaming. *A las cinco de la tarde* is the hour of our love, the hour I hold your fleshless hand in the room of specters. *A las cinco de la tarde*, the hour I always find the ring that you threw into the depths. *A las cinco de la tarde*, the hour I call you by your real name shortly before all the lilies of the field go up in smoke, before the cocks in the sky crow thrice, before you ascend and vanish in the void you came from.

In God's darkness I touched your own darkness. I saw the shattered image of time and your magical snare uncoil three times on the mythical waters of the river. In God's thick darkness, in the *noche oscura* of poetry and ecstasy, I saw your purple hair streaming. The miracle was granted us for only an instant. I just manage to touch your mortal flesh for an instant before we two dissolve in boundless space, before your shadow abandons me forever and travels afar, like the shadows of those who, holding branches, still head for the unknown Eleusian Mysteries.

We met on this earth, even more inhospitable than outer space. There will never be true compensation for our terrestrial love, neither in this nor in any other possible world. There will be no justice for those who hungered and thirsted, for those who died while waiting, those who shed tears in the great quarry of the world. Inside the huge age-old chasm I saw your purple hair streaming. No one can look at you without dying, oh you priestess of Apollo, consumed with your rage for prophecy, you who walk naked on crimson carpets and with unintelligible words bring God down to earth.

Solitary inhabitants of this earth that was abandoned ages ago, we walk slowly at a blind man's pace on its cracked surface. No trace of humans on the desolate earth, only the uncanny buzz of insects and the vigilant gaze of large nocturnal animals that look at us, immobile. On this earth on which the ancient drama of the world plays out, on this earth littered with lunar craters and chasms, I saw your purple hair streaming. Your song resounds, lifting stones into the air, making sailors go mad and leading ships to spectral seas. It lures me to where the golden masks of the dead gaze at us without seeing us and where Man, exhausted, is fed up with playing the game of eternity.

Calm down, oh tortured soul, oh earth drenched in countless tears. One night as we proceeded silently on mountains and through uninhabited forests toward that necropolis illuminated by the faint moonlight, we took the step that not even poetry allows: we saw, dreamt or invented a world more real than the hard granite of the world. Under the last glimmers of the moon, in the darkness of the abandoned buildings, I, the most miserable of mortals, saw the fossils of the early-type stars and saw your purple hair streaming. This strange poem we are writing cannot have either beginning or end.

Our room is the cabin in this ship journeying toward the unknown. I took off your clothes with trembling hands, just as one removes the clothing from a dead body. Only the sea still shines between us; between us only the sea and the night and the fog and the wind that musses up the tufts of matted hair. Under the dark mass of the glaciers that are arriving, I saw your purple hair streaming. Only the night between us and the fog and the wind that whistles in the vacant eyes of the dead, but today I touch you for the last time before the earth becomes uninhabited and God, who never begat and was never born, sends famished swarms of birds against us.

Stretching out our bony hands, we sip the remains of the soup we are sharing. The earth trembles and our feeble old bodies are crushed under the immense rocks, under the weight of the mass of snow. In the rubble of the world there still resounds the plangent drumbeat of our love, and the birds in the night that foretell the future tumble dead onto the earth. Far off, in another world, I saw in a vision your purple hair streaming. We are the last humans, we who survived by stealing the rings from the fingers of the dead, and we saw our mortal bodies revolving forever like Ixion and saw the birth and annihilation of the Earth and the stars.

In the old room of our love I raise the oil lamp high and illuminate your face—*eternal fire that, like the world, arises and subsides in measure.* But the angel of madness flutters over the earth and the birds in the night that foretell the future crash against our window pane and are crushed. Through the eternal flame that begets and devastates the world in innumerable metamorphoses, I saw your purple hair streaming. *We are one flesh with the night,* sang the Jews of Bukovina outside our window.

My love, at the foot of the mountain, exhausted, I sat down and looked deep into your large, ingenuous eyes. Between us, a road that annihilates stellar distances. We begot poems, we begot pallid children below the silver lambency of the stars. Later, darkness fell all around us in the forest of phantoms. Together we again took the rough road of exile, carrying our bitter burden among the rocks, in this forgotten corner of the earth unceasingly flogged by the storm; and we lived *senza patria* trapped in the eternal mirages of night, strangers and suppliants, like mortals in the world of the immortal, like souls wandering in an incomprehensible world that changes ceaselessly. Among the dead trees, in the stony forest of phantoms, I saw your purple hair streaming. The mountain grieves and cracks for our orphaned children who grow up in a foreign land with bitterness and tears, and since the time of Eden the enamored flowers on the cliff have been waiting for your gentle caress to cut them until they bloom in everlasting stillness.

We spent our brief life having visions. You who are still waiting for my return while walking slowly toward the distant lights of the harbors, and I who write you unanswered love letters from the other side of the sea. In the enclosure, they cut the women's hair with large rusty scissors. Stones are falling and shatter our human bones and the birds in the night that foretell the future hurl themselves against us, screaming. Among the dark branches of the river of the dead, among the falling clouds, I saw your purple hair streaming. For years we lived hidden under the rotten wood of the ships, eating mud and bare roots. They made us stand up again, they took our names, dressed us in new clothes and sent us to live again among humans. On the edge of the inhospitable new world, the inhabitants welcomed us with a volley of stones. *The ice was here, the ice was there, the ice was all around.* This is an old song of woe taught to me by sailors, those bewitched by the sea.

A stranger to the world and the flesh, I followed you to the end and together we entered the dark region of the enigma. We proceeded to the land from which no one has ever returned alive. Below the light of the moribund sun I saw your purple hair streaming. Night is falling; the heavy bells of the last days announce the last season and the birds in the night that foretell the future flutter among the blind. Midnight is the hour when invisible hands mark the doors, the fine sand of quarries penetrates deeply into the lungs and the earth vibrates with the sound of the children hammering day and night in the cellars. But the time will come when we shall cast off one by one the clothes that lie heavy on us; the time will come when we shall banish poetry itself and will remain alone, you and I, naked in front of the large mirror of the world. Oh beloved Diotima, come back to me tonight, you who bless the holy water of the Neckar River and are lost and again return untouched by death and time; you beside me, unable to sleep, you who kneel in prayer for the happiness of all creatures, for the coming of a world in which we will all sink in peace, just as the fields, valleys and innocent animals sink into God's gentle darkness.

Ever more deeply did we proceed into the dark forest, having visions. We took the rough path that leads to the immense, frozen wastelands of the North. We looked deeply into the eyes of the large Sphinx of the world with its terrifying riddle and prayed in memory of all those who died while striving to interpret it and in memory of the one who used the holy name Scardanelli. We pinned all our hopes on poetry; before I had time to learn from your lips where God lives, the earth ripped open and we were taken far off by the freezing wind coming from the cracks and ruins of language. Both humans and animals die and are continuously reborn in a tragic cycle without end, and the birds in the night that foretell the future look at us without seeing us. Under the merciful shade of the large, sick trees, behind the pitch-black foliage, I saw your purple hair streaming. *You good spirits are present, often when a sacred cloud surrounds someone,* he once wrote. So we also passed through the flames of love and death and, immersed in silent contemplation, we let our gaze wander among the holy mountains, through the valleys and over the rivers, and we dreamt of a land that lavishly bestows its fruit to everyone.

You turn the key, push the heavy door, and the riddle is solved. From our refuge at the river bank we see the last storm is arriving, but I turned the white searchlights on you, oh naked woman whose shadow I embrace with trembling hands in the drab light inside this suffocating hospice. Through the old trees shattered by the storm I saw your purple hair streaming. The grass grows once again and by dint of eternal labor Man gains the bitter Kingdom of Heaven and Susette Gontard, Diotima, waters the innocent earth with her tears. Oh you who hold in your hand the eternal, singular crystal of this unique world, and I, together with you, fearlessly march on while you pass through the pitch-black ghost-ridden night. Innumerable the paths in the woods, which we wayfarers cross in the midst of night and fog, proceeding toward the conclusion of the drama. The ashen-faced children in tatters, all the disabled and outcasts in the world, tug at our sleeves, and the terrestrial bread that is meted out is enough for everyone. *Oh you, softer than rose leaves*, oh you girl holding the lamp high, its flame illuminating our wet earth, where we happily await the end of everything.

From behind the closed curtains we saw the infernal flames that ravage the world and listened to the frightful uproar of the crowd and the sound of the window panes shattering. In the mirror of the crystal clear night, I saw your purple hair streaming. Tomorrow future generations may also mention us in the long catalog of the annihilated, tomorrow they will recognize us by the solid gold ring. Today, however, here, in our shelter, far from the rubble of the world, here in the blessed home of Ernst Zimmer, I touch your bare breasts in the trembling light; here there are only virtuous spirits and forests even darker than this terrestrial night surround us, wild with dark green foliage. *God's will be done,* you wrote on the mirror that always reflected your image. Tomorrow the wind will again strike all the clappers on the old doors and we will go elsewhere, like birds.

Now we head toward the light of the large unborn star. Me dead, and you the immortal image on the frosted glass, in the cracked mirror. There are still roads that lead to the light of the large unborn star, paths that only God opens for humans. Paths that lead far away, up to the threshold of the solitary tower where a poet once lived, gazing at the sacred void and ecstasy. Roads and rough paths in the thick forest; roads that lead to Lauffen, the birthplace to which the wayfarer always returns, striking the earth with his cane while the storm of life rages all around. *Ο κάλλιστος* κόσμος, oracle and riddle that I must solve; meanwhile at the hour of our love the large bell rings in mourning and the carpenter's hammer strikes, reshaping the world from the beginning once again. In the light of the large unborn star, I saw your purple hair streaming and the birds in the night that foretell the future flying slowly above the dead shores, there in the bosom of the pitch-black earth, where the noble Diotima lies, more beautiful than all the flowers.

You were standing at the top of the stairs like the angel. I kissed your wet eyes, darkened by the light of madness. Darkness fell and you remained naked, without your pure white mantle. I know that tomorrow our bodies will return to the earth or to the sea; but today, beneath the starry night I embrace your sorrowful shadow and with the knife of poetry cut all the terrestrial threads one by one. Blessed be the spirit that still dwells among men; blessed the bitter earth with all its white roses, the volcanoes that awaken and the frightened animals of the forest that search for shelter. Later, the veil of the temple was rent and God neglected us. We were awakened in the night by the sound of the drums. Blinded by the searchlights, I saw, before they took us forever, your purple hair streaming. Millions of hands stretch out and the blind eyes stare at us, oh you and I, all alone *beneath so many eyelids,* like God who, without touching the ground, passes weightless among us. Thus we, like Him, walk among the wild flowers of Duino, disconsolate.

Hymns and paeans in the celestial clouds that you alone listen to. I kiss your mortal hand that tightly grasps the crystal of eternal life and I slowly lift the veil that covers your face. We found ourselves in the presence of God, we two alone, living among humans. Ambulance sirens and explosions interrupt the solitary prayer of the one who burns all his writings, and your beauty, like the plangent wind that descends from the mountains, makes the lilies of the field bend. In the dazzling whiteness of the angels I saw your purple hair streaming. No one can escape from the burden of one's sorrow even if *he dwells in the uttermost parts of the sea*. Oh you shattered image of eternity passing by and losing your way together with the innumerable generations of mankind.

Like sick trees are we, with our roots in mid-air. Yet you, oh angel of the deepest sorrow, silently descend among us and with the hand of an innocent girl gently touch these broken trunks and illuminate the eternal, uncreated world *with inexhaustible oil*. The living and dead direct their gaze at the same trembling light. All the doors are opening so that those who hunger and thirst may sit at the large table, the ill in the poorhouses may hold the melted candle in their hands and hope, and the lepers of Bethany may wait for you. In the blue light of the volcanic stone, in the prophetic bay laurel leaves that cover your face, I saw your purple hair streaming. I tried to narrate a ghost story about the whistling wind in the jet-black cracks in the houses, about the hand that rings all the bells, the young girl who got lost one night in the sea, and the love-stricken one who writes this poem and searches for her, seeking help from the spirits of the waves. I don't know how to solve this riddle that I was given; on All Souls Day the poor hold the lamp high and gather the leaves scattered by the wind.

You stand immobile at the threshold, holding the lamp; I knock and enter the house and the staircase creaks under our steps. At this hour everything around us is holy: the bare rocks, the roots of the flowers and the water you fetch from the well. Beyond the dark shores of the rivers, the valleys resound with girls' wedding songs and the prayers to a God who is able to do nothing but hold the hands of the ill and is more helpless than humans. Beneath inauspicious constellations Man walks all alone, abandons his terrestrial burden like a tired, moribund animal, without the consolation of the open sky or the large starry night. Beyond the dark shores of the rivers, far from the human world, I saw your purple hair streaming. You stand immobile at the threshold, speaking in your unintelligible language, which revives the dead leaves. Oh beloved night with which I shared bread and tears, oh night that illuminates the world's sorrow and mercifully covers the doleful earth on which we lovers walk.

Beneath this poem that I am offering you lies a dark root, darker than our love, darker than life itself or death. There is no way I can cover the stellar distances that separate us this evening while the Wormwood star draws near to Earth and murderers go up the stairs. Yet you, so calm, illuminate our dark room for the last time. In the unearthly light of the lamp, I saw your purple hair streaming. Receive this poem tonight, accept this dark root that I offer you, clawing the hard earth like a blind man. Tomorrow everything will end, tomorrow I will lose you and will search for you all alone like the errant poet in the bogs or in the windswept and barren hills of Annesley.

They gave us one hour to bury the dead; the pure white bones crack in the frigid moonlight. I invoked the dark oracle and the only reply was the echo of my own voice and the sound of the viola you are playing in the depths of the earth. Your hand shakes the branches and touches the sick leaves and the fruit of the trees continuously falls onto the dead earth like the thick snow amidst us. Further off on the horizon the rose beds burn and the blind birds that foretell the future return, bewitched by the demonic dance of the trees and the nocturnal storm. Beneath the riddle of the large starry night, beyond the mysterious and invisible conjunction of the planets, I saw your purple hair streaming. Oh, you and I all alone, lost forever in the great mystery of the world and of time that crumbled, lost forever until God returns and utters the Word we are expecting.

In the boundless world with neither beginning nor end, like flowers or birds are we, oh Regine, immersed in the holy peace of the fields and in ecstasy, crossing the mouths of the darkest rivers on this boat without a rudder steered by the blind angel of the night. I never asked anything of prayer or poetry. Truly, many a time I stood immobile under your illuminated window, lamenting like Ulysses in Hades in front of the fleeting shades of the dead; meanwhile you, with a candle in your hand, were silently pleading and the gold of our impossible union was shining on your finger. In this dizzying rotation of the world that separates us forever, I saw your purple hair streaming. We stand under God's terrifying gaze, the sick flesh trembles and disintegrates, and our mortal shell dissolves under the pale starlight. Like flowers or birds are we, in the middle of the road between God and the world, oh Regine, and too little time is given to us on this earth.

Through the frosted window pane of the asylum we see the eternal rain falling. When the lights go out and in the rooms the groans of the ill reverberate and the inmates resume their quavering melody, then from far off one can hear Simurgh the eternal bird singing and you awake next to me, touching my burning forehead with your delicate hand. Through the frosted window pane of the asylum, just before the lights go out in the rooms, I saw your purple hair streaming and Simurgh, the mythical bird no one has ever seen, sings far from the world of Man. Pushing aside dark branches, beyond the root of the deepest night, we proceeded and in the confusion and fever of the vision we stay awake waiting for dawn and talk about distant places with strange names: Purkendsdorf, Kirling, Badenweiler. We talk about the eternal rain, the ill suffering from suffocating cough and tossing in their beds, and the futile hope of being cured, now when all the lights in the rooms are turned off and an entire world crumbles forever.

I wake up during the night and look at you; there is no beginning or end to your dream time, neither death nor birth. Only the calm after the storm and the soft squeaking of the cart on the desolate road while the marble women open their closed eyelids, and the veil of the mist is dispersed, and the lonely traveler takes to the road again. Crossing the dense arctic forest, in the darkness of the abandoned gold mines I saw your purple hair streaming. I hold your hand while the old earth trembles beneath our wedding bed, and the roots of the trees get tangled in our hair. You and I, the survivors of the twentieth century, lived confined in a small attic behind the staircase, spellbound by our secret love. We the survivors lived far from all humans, looking through the window at the fog and the shadow of the trees on the immobile water and the birds in the night on the turbid canals of Amsterdam. Then the third angel blew a trumpet and we emerged with white hair, already having forgotten human speech, because those who enter here abandon all hope, and tomorrow there will be no mercy for us in the world to come.

I wake up during the night to write this poem, the poem no one will ever read. It is the hour the tragic cloud passes over us, and you are sleeping next to me, beautiful and ingenuous, and the world that does not yet exist continues to revolve. Tomorrow we will be banished from the birthplace of our happiness and we will see the dead and the survivors of the camps returning, dragging huge carts in the mud. Then I will lose you, my love, definitely and forever and there will no longer be any other place where we can find refuge. Even before God said *Let there be light,* before green grass sprouted over the earth and the dark trees began to yield fruit, in this terrifying night when trumpets sounded and walls crumbled, I saw with the eyes of madness your purple hair streaming. I stand immobile at the threshold of this world which doesn't yet exist, while my futile, terrestrial cycle is coming to a close; the earth trembles under the tremendous weight of the wheels and my scrawny body is crushed. The frightening birds of the night abandon the last foliage and you arise slowly in the midst of black columns of smoke and dissolve in the heavens, and I will never be able to write this poem.

I wake up during the night and hug this tree. Under its thick foliage we are all innocent, and you even more innocent, in this hour of tears and of the darkest ecstasy, the hour when I receive the bread and wine you offer me while you sink your tragic root deeply into the dust and whisper the names of the spectral rivers of our love: *Danube, Drinos* and *Neckar,* and our canoe slowly goes down the golden waters. Far from their mysterious banks, where the song of the solitary teal still resounds, in the age-old depths of the rivers, I saw your purple hair streaming. No rower, whether mortal or immortal, ever crossed the same river twice. Only the gods, my love, lift the terrible stones, only the gods know how to deftly cast or pull the turbid veil from our eyes. The gods who remain immobile and look at us from the coastline, slowly gathering the invisible net. We the desperately poor returned from the long journey, blind, delirious, dressed only in the miserable rags of poetry, and on the way we met neither a god nor a human. *Upon reaching the sandy shore, we dragged the vessel down to the glittering sea.*

I wake up during the night and beckon to the spirits of the waves. Oh you seas and lands and stone statuettes of women crushed by time and clouds that lift me on high and destroy my every hope of salvation. I wake up during the night all alone, as usual, more alone than ever, since nothing else of poetry remains for me tonight and the wind sweeps the ashes of all magic, rituals and visions far away. Words fall, whistling into the void, the world is collapsing into chaos and your prophetic art is totally useless. *Who ever saw a lovely maiden,* the voices of the drowned resounded from the depths, and during the entire return journey I saw only the high mountains and your purple hair streaming. Only you console me, although I will never reach you, and the dead man strikes the heavy clapper while weeping. Amidst the wreckage of the world I lift the last stone and offer it to you just before I leave forever. The sublime stars that guide us are always pale and the light of this lantern is too weak to illuminate life and the poem that death is writing. This is why I turn the iron wheel of fate all by myself and call you by your biblical names—*Sifra, Ruth, Esther*; pale, sick girls, I walk together with you on the snow-clad road of martyrdom; I follow you to the end in the thick forests of Cracow until God smashes all the Scriptures and holy Tablets. This is why today I abandon the wind-swept shelter of poetry until the inverted mirror image again reflects for me your beloved image and the dead man who vanished returns among us, slowly shaking the dust off his clothes.

We removed our clothes one piece at a time and dived into the water. From on high, unconcerned about the terrestrial drama, shadows of birds cross over the immobile surface of the lake. Naked, we walked on the bare rocks, moving toward our ultimate union as far as the center of the incandescent sphere of the sun, there where bodies and souls melt like candles, and far off on the opposite shore waiting for us behind the rows of dark trees, are those who foretell the future with the black innards of birds, those who pass through the eye of a needle and pray for the fecundity of the earth; the diviners with glazed eyes who warn us with unintelligible words. *O my soul, hang your clothes on the wheel of life and death*, sang the poet in love and together with him all the flaming beings are swirling and the maidens of Tauris bathing in the sempiternal waters. Behind the rows of dark trees, in this dream that is the cosmos, even the maidens of Tauris move off and I touch the words of this poem with my mutilated hand for the last time.

I secretly meet you under the arches, under the stone bridges, oh my pale beloved, and afterward I return inconsolably to sleep in the bosom of the dark earth. We are also birds in the night, solitary, made *of one flesh* that was ruthlessly lacerated; we are dark birds that go beyond and, since the poem is written laboriously only in the shadow of death, we take the rough road that leads to the crystalline springs of life. Under the arches, under the stone bridges, processions of dancers pass with wild songs and drums. *Πολλαί μορφαί των δαιμονίων;* only with great labor, and only should some god so will it, is the poem written. Under the arches, under the stone bridges, I saw your purple hair streaming for a fleeting moment. *Io son venuto al punto de la rota,* I murmured to myself, my gaze directed at the scattered leaves you left when passing by this Earth like a cloud, the scattered leaves your grace trod so delicately while setting off.

I walked in the wasteland all alone. I walked in your terrifying solitude until I came upon the stone angel. In the muddy water of the wells, amidst myriad reflections, I saw your purple hair streaming. There will never be hope for another life for those who survived the merciless wind, the fangs of night, the embrace of mother poetry, but my love—which sings of decay and ashes and the sick world that revolves and the futility of the terrestrial—will again move the sun and the other stars.

NOTES

p. 3
Away...: Alexandros Papadiamantis, Φαρμακολύτρια
(Deliverer from Potions and Spells).

p. 8
Away, away!...: Shelley, *Stanzas.*

p. 10
Every angel is terrifying: Rilke, the first and second *Duino Elegies.*

p. 11
A las cinco de la tarde (At five in the afternoon): Federico García Lorca,
Lament for Ignacio Sánchez Mejías.

p. 12
Noche oscura (dark night): a reference to *Dark Night of the Soul*, a poem
by St. John of the Cross.

p. 17
Ixion: the Lapith king in Greek mythology who, due to his impudent
attempt to seduce Hera, was punished by being tied to a perpetually
spinning wheel of fire.

p. 18
Eternal fire…: Heraclitus, *On Nature.*

We are one flesh…: Paul Celan, *Speech-Grille.*

Bukovina: A region in Romania where Paul Celan was born and where roughly half the Jewish population was exterminated in 1941.

p. 19
Senza patria: without a homeland.

p. 20
The ice was here…: Coleridge, *Rime of the Ancient Mariner.*

p. 21
A stranger to the world and the flesh: Alexandros Papadiamantis, *Τα Πτερόεντα δῶρα* (The Flying Gifts).

Diotima: the name the German poet Heinrich Hölderlin gave to the love of his life, Susette Gontard.

p. 22
Scardanelli: one of the pseudonyms used by Hölderlin.

You good spirits…: Hölderlin, *The Source of the Danube.*

p. 23
Softer than rose leaves: Sappho, *Stand Face to Face, Friend.*

p. 24

Ernst Zimmer: a carpenter who let the poet Hölderlin live in the tower of his family residence, where he remained for the last 36 years of his life.

p. 25

Lauffen: the birthplace of Friedrich Hölderlin.

Ο κάλλιστος **κόσμος** (the most beautiful cosmos): Heraclitus, fragment 124.

p. 26

Beneath so many eyelids: from the epitaph that the poet Rainer Maria Rilke composed for himself: *Rose, oh pure contradiction, desire to be no one's sleep beneath so many eyelids.*

Duino: the castle near Trieste where Rilke began to write the *Duino Elegies*.

p. 27

He dwells…: *Psalms* 139, verse 9.

p.28

With inexhaustible oil: Rilke, *The Notebooks of Malte Laurids Brigge*.

p. 30

Hills of Annesly: Lord Byron, *Hills of Annesley*.

p. 32

Regine: Regine Olsen was philosopher Søren Kierkegaard's fiancée, who played a vital role in the development of his thought.

p. 33

Purkendsdorf, Kirling, Badenweiler: the sites of three sanatoriums in Central Europe in the early 20th century.

p. 36

Upon reaching…: Homer, *The Odyssey*, Book XI.

p. 37

Who ever saw a lovely maiden: a line from a traditional Greek poem, the story of a maiden who is brought back home by her dead brother. It is also the subject of traditional songs and poems in other Balkan countries.

p. 39

Of one flesh: Celan, *Snowbed*.

Πολλαί μορφαί των δαιμονίων (Divinity appears in many forms): Euripides, *Bacchae*.

Io son venuto… (I have come to the conjunction of the wheel): Dante, *Rime petrose*.

Stamatis Polenakis was born in Athens, Greece in 1970. He was trained as a cinema director in Athens and also studied Spanish culture and language at the Complutense University of Madrid. He has lived and worked in Spain and Ireland (Dublin). He is the author of seven poetry collections and a novel, and has also written theatrical works, four of which have been staged. In 2017 his collection *The Roses of Mercedes* was awarded the Greek National Prize for Poetry. Polenakis' poetry has been translated into English, French, Spanish, Italian, German and Slovenian.

RICHARD PIERCE is a translator and sculptor from the San Francisco Bay Area. In his early twenties he lived in Athens for four years, where he was a teacher and journalist. Since then he has lived in Verona, Italy, working initially as an English teacher, then as an editor for Mondadori Publishers, and currently as a freelance translator. In 2005 he began to translate contemporary Greek poetry and since 2010 has been translating the body of work of Stamatis Polenakis. His translations have appeared in *Poetry Review, Ars Poetica, Poem, Cross-Section, Austerity Measures,* and the online magazine *Greek Poetry Now.*